Party Time!

I Talk You Talk Press

CONTENTS

1. A FANCY DRESS

Teresa was a student from Sao Paulo. She was studying English at a language school in London. There were 20 other students in her class. Teresa wanted to talk with them, but there was a problem. She was very shy. At lunchtime, the other students all talked to each other. Their English was very good. Teresa didn't think her English was good. She wanted to talk to the other students, but she didn't have the confidence. So, she ate lunch alone.

After lunch on Thursday, the teacher said, "We are having a welcome party tomorrow night. It will be in the school cafeteria. It will start at seven pm. The students from other classes will come too."

Teresa was excited about the party, but she felt a little nervous.

What should I wear? she thought. *What do people wear to parties in England?*

The class finished at 3:00pm. The other students walked out of the classroom. They were all talking about the party and laughing. The teacher was cleaning the board.

I'll ask the teacher, thought Teresa.

"Excuse me Ms Mills, can I ask you about the party?"

"Sure," said Ms Mills.

"What should I wear?"

"Wear something fancy. Everyone usually dresses up at the parties," said Ms Mills.

"Something fancy?"

"Yes. A fancy dress."

"OK, thank you. I will."

"Good! See you tomorrow!" said Ms Mills.

Teresa walked out of the school and got on the bus to go back to her apartment.

Ms Mills said wear something fancy. Everyone usually dresses up. What does fancy mean? Teresa had been too shy to ask. She looked it up on her smartphone.

Fancy…ah, fancy dress! People wear costumes! I've seen fancy dress parties in movies. They look fun! So, it is a fancy dress party! What can I wear?

Teresa looked out of the bus window and thought about the party. *A fancy dress party is a good idea,* she thought. *People will talk to each other about their costumes. If I wear an interesting costume, maybe I can make lots of friends. First, I need to hire a costume.*

She found the address of a fancy dress costume shop on her smartphone. It was about a 20 minute walk from her apartment. She got off the bus and walked to the shop.

In the shop window, there were many kinds of costumes. There were animal costumes, Disney costumes, Halloween costumes, and many others.

She opened the door and went into the shop.

"Can I help you?" asked the woman behind the counter.

"Yes, I'm looking for a fancy dress costume."

"What kind of costume would you like?"

"I don't know."

The woman looked at Teresa. "How about Snow White from the Disney movies?"

Teresa thought about it. "OK. Can I try it on?" she asked.

The woman brought Teresa the Snow White dress. She went into the changing room and put the dress on. She looked in the mirror.

"I don't know," she said. "It's a little too big."

"OK," said the woman. "How about a tiger? We have a tiger costume. It is the perfect size for you."

Teresa tried on the tiger costume. It fitted perfectly. She smiled at herself in the mirror.

She looked like a tiger! "Yes, I'll wear this."

"When is your party?"

"Tomorrow night."

"OK. Well, you must bring this back on Saturday morning before lunchtime," said the woman.

"OK, thank you," said Teresa.

Teresa paid and walked out of the shop with the tiger costume in a bag. She walked back to her apartment and made some pasta for dinner.

After dinner, she put the costume on. She looked in the mirror and laughed.

I hope I can make friends with the other students tomorrow night, she thought.

Teresa studied hard on Friday. After school, she got the bus back to her apartment and started to get ready. She looked at herself in the mirror before she left her apartment.

I'm a tiger, so I have to be strong! I have to be confident and talk to many people! she thought.

Teresa smiled and left her apartment at 6:15pm.

I have to get the bus! she thought. *The driver will think I am very strange.* As she walked through the streets, many people looked at her. Some people smiled. Teresa smiled back. The driver of the bus smiled too.

"Fancy dress party?" he asked.

"Yes," she said.

"Good costume!" said the driver.

"Thanks!" said Teresa.

This was a good idea, she thought. *People are smiling and talking to me. Maybe I can make friends with the students at the language school.*

Teresa got off the bus near the school. She saw some other students going into the school.

They are in my class, she thought. *But, that's strange…why aren't they wearing costumes?*

One of the students was wearing a beautiful red dress, and the man with her was wearing a suit.

Teresa walked into the cafeteria.

What!? she thought.

All the women were wearing normal dresses and the men were wearing smart shirts and trousers. No one else was wearing a costume!

Teresa wanted to run away, but it was too late. People were looking at her. Then, people started to smile. Some people laughed.

Ms Mills saw Teresa and ran over to her.

"Teresa! What are you doing?" she asked.

"You said wear something fancy, so I thought it was a fancy dress

3

party," said Teresa.

"Oh no! I'm so sorry Teresa! 'Fancy' is an adjective. It means elegant and nice. But you are right. 'Fancy dress party' means a costume party. It is not very clear. 'A fancy dress' means 'an elegant dress'. 'Fancy dress' means 'a costume'. I'm sorry, I didn't explain very well. I should have explained clearly."

Teresa wanted to cry. Just then, a few students walked over to them. One of the students, Jose, put a drink in Teresa's hand. "This is for you, Tiger!" he said.

Olga, another student, pulled Teresa onto the dance floor. "Come on! Let's dance!"

Teresa danced with the other students.

"You are so cool!" said Jose. "In class you seem very quiet, but you are really fun!"

"Yes," said Olga. "I thought you were shy, but you came here in a tiger costume! I love it!"

Teresa laughed. "Actually, I am shy. I made a mistake."

Jose shook his head. "Don't worry about it! It's a great mistake!"

They danced to a few more songs, and then they went over to the table with the food.

"Let's eat," said Jose. "I'm really hungry."

"What do tigers eat?" asked Olga.

"I don't know. But this tiger is going to have some chocolate cake!" said Teresa.

Everyone laughed.

Teresa had a great time. Everyone wanted to know why she was wearing a tiger costume. She talked to many people and made lots of friends that night. She danced and drank and ate, and laughed a lot.

At the end of the night, Ms Mills said, "I'm sorry Teresa. But I hope you had a good time."

"Oh it's OK," said Teresa. "Actually, I'm glad. I'm very shy, and it is difficult for me to talk to people. But everyone was so nice and friendly. They all wanted to talk to me! Thanks to the costume, I could make many new friends!"

2. THE HEN PARTY

One Monday, my friend Maddy and I were eating lunch in the park when Barbara came over to our bench. "Can I join you?" she asked.

Maddy didn't answer. She didn't like Barbara very much. Barbara came to work in our office about three months ago. She is very beautiful. Everyone knows that she got the job because she is engaged to Drew Lawrence, the coolest guy in the office. Drew got promoted to office manager and within a week, Barbara arrived. This made Maddy angry. She liked Drew Lawrence a lot and she hoped that he would ask her out on a date sometime. Barbara didn't talk to anyone in the office. Everyone thought she was very proud.

"We're not good enough for her," they said. "She thinks she is better than us because she is the boss's girlfriend."

"Is it OK?" asked Barbara again. "Can I sit with you?"

"Sure," I said to Barbara. "Move along," I told Maddy. "Make room for Barbara."

Maddy moved along, and Barbara sat down between us. Maddy and I waited for Barbara to speak, but she didn't say anything.

I looked at Barbara. She is stunning! I thought. *I'm not surprised that Drew wants to marry her.* But Barbara didn't look happy. Her face was red and she was looking down at her hands.

"Is there something you wanted to talk about, Barbara?" I asked.

"Mmm. Yes. But it's so embarrassing," answered Barbara. "Drew and I are getting married in two weeks. He is having a pre-wedding party with his friends this weekend. He's having a guys' party."

"A stag party?" I asked.

"Yes. A stag party. They are going to go fishing, then bowling and then they will go to a pub and all get drunk," explained Barbara.

"So why is it embarrassing?" asked Maddy. Maddy didn't like Barbara, but this was interesting.

"Well. Drew's mother and sisters keep asking me about my 'girls night out', my hen party. They expect me to have a big evening out with my girlfriends. Drew's sisters want to be invited."

"So what's the problem?" asked Maddy. "Your bridesmaids will arrange it. You just tell them to invite Drew's sisters."

Barbara started to cry.

"I only planned to have one bridesmaid. I asked my younger sister to be my bridesmaid. She lives in France, but she was going to come back last month and stay with me until the wedding day. But she broke her leg and is still in hospital."

"Why don't you ask one of your friends to arrange your party?" I asked.

Barbara cried even more. She was crying quite loudly. "I don't have any friends!"

Maddy didn't like Barbara very much, but she is a very kind person. She found some tissues in her handbag and gave them to Barbara. She patted Barbara on the back.

"What would you like Kirstie and me to do?" she asked. "Do you want us to arrange your hen party?"

"No, no," said Barbara. "I will do that. I will plan everything. I just want you to come to the party. I want you to pretend to be my friends. I don't want Drew's family to know that I don't have any friends."

"OK," said Maddy. "Kirstie and I will come. Won't we Kirstie?"

"Yes, of course," I said. "But Barbara. Can I ask you a question?"

Barbara looked at me. "Yes. What do you want to know?"

"Why don't you talk to anyone in our office?" I asked.

"I didn't want to work in your office. I knew it was a very bad idea. I told Drew it was a mistake but he said there would be no problem. He was wrong. Everyone hates me!"

"Oh, that's not true!" I said.

But Maddy was more honest. "Barbara. You don't talk to anyone. So people think you are very proud. People think you believe you are better than them."

Barbara nodded. "I understand what you are saying. But I am very shy. And I saw how people looked at me the first day I came to the office. I was the boss's girlfriend, so of course they wouldn't like me."

"Try to be friendlier to people," said Maddy. "Try to talk more. And Kirstie and I will come to your pre-wedding party."

"Thank you!" said Barbara. "It will be on Saturday night. I'll tell you all about it when I finish making a plan."

Barbara tried hard to talk to people in the office. Everyone was surprised. But they started saying, "Maybe she's not so bad." And they started to like her a little more. Barbara was excited about the party. On Thursday she asked Maddy and I to go to lunch with her.

"We'll go to the new pizza restaurant. My treat!" she said.

We ordered our pizzas and while we were waiting, Barbara said, "I have something else to ask you."

"What's that?" asked Maddy.

"My sister can't come to the wedding. She will be in hospital for two or three more weeks. So I want to ask you, Maddy, to be my bridesmaid. I would like to ask both of you, but there is only one dress. And Kirstie, I'm sorry. You are so tall and slim. The dress would never fit you. But I want you to come to the wedding too."

"It's OK," I answered. "I would spoil the photographs. I would be taller than everyone including the bridegroom."

"Are you sure?" asked Barbara.

"Yes, I'm sure," I said. "But I would like to go to the wedding."

"So, Maddy." Barbara turned to Maddy. "Would you please be my bridesmaid?"

Maddy looked serious. "What's the dress like?"

"My sister bought it in France. I haven't seen it yet. Her roommate is sending it by courier. You are about the same size as her, but it will probably be too long. We can get it made shorter next week."

"Do you know what colour it is?" asked Maddy.

"It's green. A kind of turquoise colour. And it's long, and it's strapless."

Maddy smiled. "It sounds OK. If it fits me, I'll be your bridesmaid. Though I'm sorry Kirstie can't be a bridesmaid too."

"Don't worry about me!" I said. "I'll be looking around the wedding guests to find the man of my dreams. You will have to dance with the best man."

Barbara laughed. "The best man is Dayton Willing."

I laughed too. Dayton Willing is about forty years old. He's short and bald.

"Dayton Willing! Oh no!" said Maddy. "I hope the dress is beautiful!"

Our pizzas arrived and while we ate Barbara told us about the plans for Saturday. "We'll start at my apartment with cocktails. Then I've booked a champagne dinner on a cruise boat."

"A cruise boat!" shouted Maddy and I.

"The boat that does cruises for tourists along the river. They have a Saturday night special. Then after that, we'll go to a nightclub. So wear something sparkly. We're going to shine!"

On Saturday night Maddy and I took the bus to Barbara's apartment. I was wearing my best black hipster trousers and a short sparkly bright green top. Maddy was wearing her favourite party dress. It's silver and very short. She was carrying a department store bag. "What's that?" I asked.

"It's a present for Barbara. My brother Colin made it."

"Can I see it?" I asked. Colin is very clever. But he makes crazy things. He once made me a Christmas tree hat with a flashing star on top.

"No," said Maddy. "It's a surprise."

When we got to the apartment we rang the doorbell. We waited a long time for Barbara to answer the door. When she finally opened the door, we got a shock. She was wearing pyjamas and an old sweatshirt. Her face was red and swollen. She looked like she had been crying for hours.

"Barbara!" I said. "Why aren't you ready? It's party time!"

Maddy walked into the apartment and put her arms around Barbara. "What's wrong?"

"There is no party," said Barbara.

"Sit down and tell us what's happened," said Maddy.

We sat down in Barbara's tiny living room. Barbara explained.

"The party was going to be very small; just you two, and Drew's two sisters and Drew's cousin. But I thought it would be OK. But his sisters found out that my sister couldn't come to the wedding. They thought that one of them should be bridesmaid instead. When I told them I had asked Maddy to be bridesmaid, they all got angry. So they called this morning and said they wouldn't come to the party!"

Maddy and I were shocked. *Poor Barbara!* we thought.

We all sat in silence for a while. Then Maddy jumped up. "Barbara! Come with me! You need makeup. And what were you going to wear? We might only be three people but we will have a great party! Kirstie, you make us some cocktails!"

Barbara had bought party food and ingredients for cocktails. I found them all in the kitchen. Barbara had printed a recipe for pineapple margaritas from the Internet. So I made one for each of us and put nuts and crackers into little bowls.

By the time I finished, Barbara and Maddy were back in the living room. Barbara looked much better although her eyes were still swollen. She was wearing silver sandals with very high heels and a bright blue dress. I handed them their cocktails.

"A toast," said Maddy. "A toast to the best hen party ever!"

We all sipped our cocktails and Barbara smiled. "You really are the best friends I've ever had, even if you are only pretending for tonight!"

"What do you mean, 'pretending'?" I said. "After all of this, we will be friends for life!"

Barbara cried again, but this time they were happy tears.

"Thank you both", she said.

The champagne dinner on the cruise boat was wonderful. When the waiter brought the champagne, Maddy handed the plastic bag to Barbara. "This is for you! You are a princess tonight!"

Barbara opened the bag. Colin had made a crown. It was silver and he had put tiny lights all around it. Maddy leant over and turned on the tiny battery pack. The lights flashed on and off. They spelt the word 'bride'.

Barbara put the crown on – it looked crazy, but it looked amazing too.

She was still wearing the crown when we left the boat and walked to the nightclub.

The nightclub was very dark and very noisy. A local band was playing. They were very good. We got asked to dance by a lot of different guys. All the guys wanted to dance with Barbara. They didn't seem to mind that she was wearing a crown with lights on it that spelt 'bride'. I was not surprised. She looked so beautiful and so happy. Everyone I danced with was shorter than me, but that was OK. I'm used to it.

At 2:00 am the band played their last tune. Everyone jumped up and down and waved their arms in the air and shouted. Then the lights came on. I looked around for Maddy and Barbara. It was time to go home. That was when I saw him. It sounds silly to say 'the man of my dreams'. But that's what it was like. He was very tall, blond and very good looking. And he was walking towards me!

"Are you Kirstie?" he asked.

"Uh, yes."

I felt breathless. He was at least 15cm taller than me, and he was so good looking. He had a nice voice too.

"How do you know my name?" I asked.

"I'm Paul. Barbara's brother. She told me about you and Maddy. She told me to look for you because you would be the tallest woman here." he smiled. "She also told me that I would like you a lot."

"But why are you here?" I asked.

I felt stupid. The man of my dreams was standing next to me and I was asking such a stupid question!

Paul didn't seem to notice. "Barbara asked me to come and pick you up. She thought it might be difficult to find a taxi," he said.

Barbara and Maddy came running up.

"Paul. This is Maddy. And I see you found Kirstie," said Barbara.

"Yes," said Paul. "You told me she was tall, with long dark blonde hair. But you didn't tell me she was beautiful!"

I stopped breathing. *This gorgeous man thinks I'm beautiful!*

"Do you like my crown?" laughed Barbara.

The lights were still flashing on and off.

Paul laughed too. "It suits you. You should wear it to the wedding."

The wedding, I thought. *Maddy will be the bridesmaid, but I will be at the wedding and so will Paul. This might have been the smallest hen party ever, but it has also been the best hen party ever!*

3. THE BIRTHDAY PARTY

"I won't do it!" shouted Mark. "I won't take Stevie to the party!"

Mark's mother folded her arms and looked at him. Mark sighed. He was 25 years old. He owned a successful software company. But when his mother looked at him like that, he felt about 10 years old.

"Your brother-in-law is in hospital. Your sister is at the hospital with him. Stevie is only five years old. This is the first time he has been invited to a birthday party. He is very excited. He can't go alone, and your father and I are busy," said his mother.

"But I have plans! I'm going to watch the soccer match with my friends, and then we are going to the pub!"

"You can give up one Saturday afternoon for your nephew!" said his mother.

Mark gave up. "OK! OK! I'll do it! I just take him to the house, and then go later and pick him up, right?"

Mark was thinking that he could still spend some time with his friends.

"No," answered his mother. "The children are all very young. You have to stay at the party. They will have some food and coffee for the parents. It will finish at four thirty, so you'll still be able to go to the pub."

"OK. I'll do it." *I can never win when my mother decides I should do something. Even if I don't want to,* thought Mark.

"Good," said his mother. "Stevie is helping your father clean the garage. I'll give him some lunch and get him dressed in his favourite clothes. You should leave here about one thirty. The party starts at two o' clock. You can take my car. Stevie's safety seat will never fit in that sports car of yours."

At 1:30pm, Mark strapped Stevie into his safety seat. Stevie was very excited. "I have a present, Uncle Mark! Mum and I bought a present for Colby! Do you want to see it?"

Stevie was holding a box wrapped in bright paper. There was an envelope taped to the outside of the box.

"No, Stevie. You give it to Colby. If we look now, we will spoil the wrapping paper," said Mark.

"I got a card too! It's got a racing car on it! I wrote on the card. I wrote 'Happy birthday Colby'! Mum wrote it down for me and I copied it. And I wrote my name! I wrote 'from Stevie'. Mum didn't write Stevie for me to copy. I can write my name! It's S...T...E..."

"Yeah, yeah, Stevie," said Mark. "I know. Now please be quiet for a bit. I have to drive."

Oh, no, thought Mark. *Stevie is a cute kid and I love him. But a whole afternoon of five-year-olds? Do they all talk this much? I'll go crazy.*

Mark had trouble finding Colby's house. When he finally found it, it was five past two. It was a very big house with double gates. The gates were open and he drove down a long driveway and parked outside the house. There were ten or more cars parked there.

Wow, thought Mark. *These people must have a lot of money! The house and gardens are huge!*

He got out of the car and opened the door to unstrap Stevie from his seat. He lifted Stevie out and they walked together towards the front door. Stevie looked up at the house and stopped walking.

"I want to go home," he said. "I don't like this house."

Mark looked down at Stevie. He was wearing a T-shirt with a hippopotamus on it, and jeans and sneakers. His blond hair was smooth and shiny, but his face was red, and his brown eyes were filled with tears.

Mark crouched down next to Stevie. "It will be OK, Stevie," he said. "Don't you want to see Colby and the other kids from school?"

"The house is scary!" said Stevie.

"No, no. It's not scary. It's Colby's house. Come on. Let's go inside."

"Will you stay with me?" asked Stevie.

"Of course I'll stay with you," answered Mark.

Mark found some tissues in his pocket and wiped Stevie's tears away. He stood up and took Stevie's hand. They walked up the steps towards the front door.

It was open. They went inside. There was a table with party hats, name tags and small plastic bags on it. Everything had the name of a child on it. Mark and Stevie found the hat, name tag and plastic bag that were labelled 'Stevie'. Stevie looked inside the plastic bag. "There's a cup inside, Uncle Mark! It has my name on it too!"

"That's great Stevie," said Mark. "I think I have to wear a name tag too."

Mark looked at the plain white name tags for adults. He found one with his sister's name, 'Michelle Beavis, mother of Stevie'. He took a pen out of his pocket and crossed out the words. He wrote 'Mark Taylor, uncle of Stevie'. He stuck the label on his shirt.

Mark looked around the front hall of the house. To the right was a pair of double doors. There was a lot of noise coming from behind the doors.

"The party's over in that room," he told Stevie. Stevie looked nervous again. "Come on Stevie. It'll be OK," said Mark. He took his nephew's hand and they walked over to the room. Mark opened the door and they went in. It was very noisy. There were children running and shouting. In one corner there were a group of adults talking loudly to each other.

Mark saw a table covered with presents. "We'll take your present to that table over there," he said pointing.

"But Uncle Mark, I want to give it to Colby!" Stevie didn't understand.

"Later on, Colby will open all his presents at the same time. Look, the other children have put their presents there."

"OK." Stevie went over to the table and put his present next to the others.

"Stevie!" A thin boy with red hair and glasses ran up to Stevie. "We're going to have food and a magician and games!" said the boy. He ran back towards the group of shouting children and Stevie followed him.

Mark walked over to the corner where the adults were standing. There was a table for self-service tea and coffee. He served himself coffee and relaxed. A dark-haired woman wearing a green dress came over to Mark.

"Who are you with?" she asked.

"Stevie Beavis," answered Mark.

"But you're not Stevie's father! I know him." The woman was puzzled.

"No. I'm his uncle." Mark pointed to his name tag. "Bill is in hospital and Michelle, my sister, is with him. There was no one else to bring Stevie to the party. That's why I'm here."

"Oh, no! What is wrong with Bill? Will he be OK?" asked the woman.

"He cut his hand badly at work. But, yes, I'm sure he will be OK."

"I'm Christine, by the way," said the woman. "My daughter's April. That's her over there." She pointed to a small girl wearing a pink party dress in the middle of the group of children.

A bell rang loudly. The children stopped shouting and running, and the adults stopped talking.

A very beautiful young woman wearing black pants and a white shirt stepped into the middle of the room. "It's time for the fun to begin!" she said. "My name is Salima. We will have games, and then we will have afternoon tea. Then Colby will open his presents and we will have birthday cake. But before we start, let's all say happy birthday to Colby!"

"Happy birthday, Colby," shouted all the children and adults. All the parents at the party were very friendly. They all talked to Mark, but they talked about the teachers at the children's school, house prices, and children's sports competitions. Mark was rather bored so he watched the children instead.

The children played games. They popped balloons by sitting on them, they had a popcorn relay and a 'guess what's in the parcel' game. Salima organised everything. Mark noticed that all the children won a prize for something. He thought Salima was very clever. He also noticed that she was very pretty.

Mark thought it was strange. He was sure that Salima was Indian but Colby was red-haired. *Perhaps Colby's father isn't Indian,* he thought. *I wonder where he is.*

Christine was standing next to him. "Colby's mother is very young, isn't she?" Mark said to Christine.

"Colby's mother isn't here," said Christine. "His father's not here either."

Mark was shocked. "Poor Colby. Doesn't he have any parents?"

"Oh, yes. He has parents. They are both very famous lawyers.

They are both away on business."

"Poor little boy," said Mark. He thought it was terrible.

"It is bad, isn't it?" said Christine. "His parents are both very nice people but they are so busy. They try hard to make sure that one of them is always here for Colby, but this time it didn't work out. His babysitter is here somewhere and his mother is trying to get back by early evening. But he seems happy, doesn't he?"

Mark looked across the room at Colby. Colby was sitting on a balloon trying to make it pop. "Yes he does look happy but I still think it's a pity. So who is Salima?"

"Salima? Oh, the young woman who is running the party? She's from the party planning company," said Christine.

"A party planning company? What's that?"

"Well you know about wedding planners?" asked Christine.

"Yes," answered Mark.

"Well, it's the same thing. You contact the company and you give them the names and ages of the children who are coming to the party. You tell them the theme you want – for example, animals, cars, fairies, Harry Potter… Then they do everything. They supply hats, gift bags, the prizes, the food, and the cake. They send someone to organize the games. The parents don't have to do anything. Of course they are very expensive."

"Do you use a children's party planner?" Mark asked Christine.

"Oh, no," she laughed. "It's very expensive and anyway, I like arranging parties for April and my other children! But Colby's parents are very busy people and they have a lot of money."

It was time for afternoon tea. Mark noticed that the food was the same as he used to have when he was a child. There were tiny sandwiches, mini meat pies and sausages. There were small iced cakes and fruit and ice cream. The children drank fruit juice.

Waitresses arrived from the kitchen with sandwiches, cookies and fresh jugs of coffee for the adults.

Mark watched Salima. *So she isn't Colby's mother,* he thought. *Maybe she isn't married. She looks very young and she is the prettiest woman here. She seems very nice and she is good with the children. I'm sure she's smart too.*

It was time for the presents and the cake. All the children were excited and happy. Mark was still watching Salima. *I'd like to ask her out on a date. Maybe when the party is finished I can talk to her. I hope she doesn't have a boyfriend. But someone as cute as that is sure to have a boyfriend.*

The party was finally over. All the children put their prizes from the games into their little plastic bags. There were other little presents for each child too and a slice of birthday cake. Salima disappeared for a moment and came back with a balloon for each child.

Stevie came looking for Mark. "Uncle Mark! It was a good party and Colby liked my present!"

"That's good Stevie! And now it's time to go home," said Mark.

"OK," said Stevie. Mark was surprised. He thought Stevie would want to stay. He looked down at Stevie. *He's very tired,* thought Mark. *It's been a busy afternoon for a small boy.* Then Mark had an idea.

"We'll go now, Stevie. But before we leave, I think you should go and say thank you to Salima."

"Salima?" Stevie was puzzled.

"The party lady. Her name is Salima. You should say thank you to her."

"OK," said Stevie. "She's nice. Colby's mother's nice too but she's not here today. She's busy."

Stevie walked over to Salima, Mark followed him. *This is my chance!* thought Mark.

Salima was taking the plates and glasses off the table. "Thank you!" said Stevie. "Thank you for the party!"

Salima looked down at Stevie and smiled. "You're welcome," she said. "Did you have a nice time?"

"Yes," said Stevie. "And I won a little car. I was in the best team for the popcorn relay."

"I'm sure you were very good," said Salima.

Mark was waiting for his chance. "I'm Mark. Mark Taylor. I'm Stevie's uncle. You did a great job today."

"Thank you."

"Do you do this every day? Do you have another party to arrange tonight?" asked Mark.

"No. I'm a student. I do this as a part-time job. Just children's parties on Saturday and Sunday afternoons," said Salima.

"Are you studying to be a teacher? I am sure you would be very good!"

Mark was talking a lot. He wanted to find out everything about Salima. He wanted her to come on a date with him.

"No. I am studying computer science," she said.

"I have a software company. We should talk some more. Let me help you tidy up here. I can carry plates and glasses for you."

Salima laughed. "Thank you for the offer. But you have a very tired little boy standing next to you. I think you should take him home."

Mark had forgotten about Stevie. He looked down. Poor Stevie. Mark felt bad. "Yes, you're right. I will take him home. But I would like to talk to you. Are you free tonight?"

"Maybe," said Salima. "What is your idea?"

"Can I take you out for dinner?" he asked.

"No. I won't finish here for another two hours or more and I will be tired. But I will meet you for a drink if you like. Just for an hour. I have to study tomorrow."

Mark arranged to meet Salima in the local pub at 8:00pm. He took Stevie out to the car and strapped him into his safety seat. He got into the driver's seat and drove down the long driveway to the gate.

"Did you like the party?" he asked Stevie.

"Yes. Best party," answered Stevie sleepily.

"Yes I think so too," Mark told Stevie. "Don't tell your mother or your grandmother, but I think it was the best party ever."

4. BECKY'S PARTY

Becky was excited. Her parents planned to go away for the weekend. It was their wedding anniversary, so they were going to a resort on the Gold Coast.

Becky was sitting in a cafe having lunch with her friends from college.

"So, you have the house to yourself all weekend! Lucky you!" said her friend Alison.

"Yeah, I can't wait! No one to tell me to wash the dishes, no one to tell me to clean my room...peace and quiet for a whole weekend!" said Becky.

"Why don't you have a party at your house?" asked Alison.

"A party at my house? That's a good idea," said Becky.

"Yeah, it doesn't have to be a big party," said Celine. "Just a small party, with a few friends."

"Yeah, let's do it Becky!" said Alison.

"OK, yeah! Saturday night will be good," said Becky. "I'll email everyone later."

"Why don't you just create an event on Facebook? You can make an event page, and invite your friends. It's easier and quicker than emailing everyone," said Celine.

"Good idea!" said Becky.

Later that day, Becky made an event page and sent Facebook invitations to her party to her friends. She wrote:

--- *My parents are away for the weekend so I'm having a party at my house on Saturday. It will start at 7:30. Bring your own food and drink! Let's have fun!* ---

On Friday morning, after breakfast, Becky's mother said, "Are you sure you will be OK on your own?"

"I'll be fine, mum. I'm eighteen. I'm an adult now!"

"Yes, well, be careful. Make sure you lock the doors when you go out. I've told the neighbours that we are going away for a few days."

"It's OK! I'll be fine. I'll just study. I have tests at college next week. You have a nice time."

"We will," said Becky's father. "We'll call you when we arrive at the hotel, and then we'll call you on Saturday and then on Sunday before we come back."

"You worry too much! Go!" said Becky.

She watched her mother and father get into the car and drive away down the street.

She smiled. *The party is going to be great!* she thought.

All day Saturday, Becky prepared for the party. She bought lots of snacks - crisps, cakes, chocolate, and some beer. *Everyone I invited is over eighteen, so we are all old enough to drink,* she thought.

She had a bath, and put on her new black dress. She put her make up on. She smiled at herself in the mirror. *I look like a nice party hostess,* she thought. She put some pop music on the stereo, opened a can of beer, and danced around the living room.

At 7:30pm, the doorbell rang. She opened the door. "Hi Celine! Hi Alison! And...er...are these your friends?" She looked at the two girls behind Celine and Alison.

Alison shook her head. They walked into the house. "I don't know who they are," whispered Alison. "Did you invite them?"

Becky shook her head.

"Hi girls," she said. "Do I know you?"

"Hi," said one of the girls. "We haven't met, but we are friends with Kesha, from college."

"Kesha?" said Becky. Kesha wasn't Becky's friend.

"Yeah, Kesha. She will be here soon," said one of the girls.

"But I didn't invite Kesha..." said Becky.

"No? Well, she is coming anyway. Where are the drinks?"

The girls walked into the kitchen.

"Wait..." started Becky. Just then, the doorbell rang.

Five of Becky's friends arrived.

"Hi! Thanks for inviting us Becky. This is gonna be a great party!"

said Vicky. They walked into the living room, took some cans of beer out of their bags and started to drink.

"We brought some peanuts! Help yourself!" said Vicky. She put two big bags of peanuts on the table.

Then, some more people came into the house. It was a group of young men.

Becky and her friends looked at each other.

"Who are they?" asked Celine.

"I don't know," said Becky. She was starting to feel worried.

She walked over to the men. "Who are you?" she asked.

"Who are we? We are the party boys!" said one of the men. The other men laughed.

"Who invited you?" she asked.

"Who invited us? You did of course," said the man.

"I didn't invite you," said Becky. "I don't even know you!"

"You did! We got your invitation on Facebook!" They walked into the kitchen.

Then, Becky heard a noise outside. She ran to the window.

"Oh no!" she shouted.

"What is it?" asked Alison. She ran to the window too.

There was a group of young people and they were talking, singing and drinking. They looked like they were going to a football game.

"Where are they going?" said Becky.

"It looks like they are coming here!" said Alison.

"But there are around sixty people! I only invited twenty friends on Facebook!"

"So what happened?" asked Alison.

"I don't know…"

"Er, Becky, did you make the Facebook event page 'private'?" asked Celine.

Becky was quiet for a few seconds, and then she said, "Oh no…I didn't check…"

Celine looked at the page on her smart phone. "Er, Becky this is bad news. You set the page to 'public'. The party information has been shared over a hundred times…"

Just then, the crowd of people came into the house. They were talking loudly and drinking. Some of them were smoking. Then, another group of people started walking up the road.

A man who lived across the road came out of his house. He ran over to Becky's house.

"What's going on?" he shouted.

But he couldn't get in the house because now it was full, with over a hundred people. There were more people in the front garden. He called the police on his mobile phone.

Becky wanted to cry.

"What am I going to do?" she said.

Then, she heard something smash in the dining room. She ran to the dining room. Someone had fallen into the cabinet and all the glasses, cups, plates and dishes were smashed. Then someone turned the music up very loudly.

She heard someone upstairs, so she ran upstairs. She found a group of young people sitting on her parents' bed. They were drinking wine.

"Oh look!" said one of the girls. "I spilt some wine! But that doesn't matter!"

Everyone started laughing. There was red wine all over Becky's parents' bed and the carpet.

"Get out of my house!" shouted Becky. "Get out!"

The people just looked at her and started to laugh.

Just then, Becky heard a police car. She ran downstairs. Two police officers were walking into the house.

"Is this your house?" asked one of the police officers.

"Yes, it is. Please help," said Becky. "I only wanted a small party but all these people came and..." She started to cry.

It took the police an hour to get everyone out of the house. By the time everyone had left, the house was a mess.

Becky and Celine walked through the house. Alison wasn't there. She had left with someone. There were smashed glasses and cups in the dining room. There was food and drink all over the kitchen floor. There were empty beer cans in the garden. Upstairs, there were empty wine bottles and red wine all over the bedroom carpet. Becky was still crying.

"What am I going to do?" she cried.

"We have to clean up," said Celine. "Come on."

They spent all night cleaning up. They finished cleaning at 4am.

The next day, Becky's parents came back early. They were supposed to come back in the evening, but the police had called them. They came back in the morning. They were very angry.

"I can't believe you did this Becky," said her mother. "What were you thinking?"

"I'm sorry," said Becky. "I wanted to have a small party, but I made the event page 'public' on Facebook by accident…"

"How could you be so stupid?" asked her father.

"We wouldn't have minded if it was just a party with a few friends. But there is a lot of damage, and the police came, and you caused trouble for the neighbours," said her mother.

"I'm sorry!" said Becky. "I really am. I ruined your weekend. I'm so sorry. I will get a part-time job and use the money to pay for the damage."

"I think that's a good idea. If you do that, it will show us that you are growing up," said her father.

The next day, Becky had lunch with Celine and Alison. Alison was talking about a guy she had met at the party.

"I had a great time at the party," said Alison. "I met a great guy."

Becky and Celine were angry.

"It was terrible!" says Celine. "The police came and there was a lot of damage. Becky is in a lot of trouble."

"Oh, I'm sure it's not so bad," said Alison.

"OK, the next party is at your house," said Celine.

"Oh no. I can't have a party. My parents would never let me do that!" said Alison.

5. TREVOR'S RETIRMENT PARTY

Trevor was looking forward to his retirement.

Just one more week, he thought. *And then I'm free. I can relax at last.*

Trevor had been working for his company for 35 years. He had started as a junior clerk, and now he was one of the managers. Everyone liked Trevor. He was a very kind and gentle man.

It was lunch time. Trevor and some of the workers were eating their lunch in the office.

"We will be very sad to see you go," said Sven as he ate his sandwich.

"Yes, we'll miss you," said Clare.

"I'll miss you all too. And I'll miss working here," said Trevor. This was true. Trevor was happy to stop working, but he would miss his friends.

"Your retirement party will be great," said Clare. "We have been planning it for weeks."

"Oh, you are very kind," said Trevor. "But I don't want a big party…"

"Of course you do!" said Sven. "Your retirement day is a special day in your life. So you will have a big party!"

"Oh, I don't know…" said Trevor. But secretly, Trevor was pleased. He was looking forward to his party. He was looking forward to seeing everyone, and he wanted to make a speech. He wanted to tell everyone how much he liked them, and he wanted to say 'thank you' to the company president.

"Don't forget Trevor. It's on Friday night, at seven o' clock. We reserved a large party room at the Grand Hotel," said Clare.

"The Grand Hotel. That's nice," said Trevor.

"The food will be great!" said Sven.

"Yes," said Trevor. "I heard that the food in the Grand Hotel is excellent."

For the next few days, everyone in the office planned for the party. The company planned to give Trevor a gold watch, but his friends also bought small presents to give him. They hired a professional photographer for the night. Everything was going well until Wednesday morning.

When Sven got to work on Wednesday, he found Lena, one of the directors, standing in the middle of the office. Lena looked upset. When the other workers arrived, she said, "Good morning, everyone. I have some bad news. Trevor is in hospital."

"Pardon?" said Clare. "Did you say he's in hospital?"

"Yes, I did," said Lena.

"But why? What happened?" asked Sven.

"Last night, Trevor was painting his kitchen and he fell off the ladder. He hurt his back, so his wife took him to hospital."

"Will he be OK?" asked Clare.

"Oh yes. He'll be fine. The doctors want to do some tests. So, he has to stay in hospital for a week," said Lena.

"A week? But, what about his party?" asked Miles, one of the other workers.

"I'm afraid he won't be able to come to his party," said Lena. "We will have to cancel it."

Everyone was very shocked. They were all very quiet that morning. No one wanted to talk.

At lunchtime, Clare said, "I'm going to the hospital. I want to see Trevor. I'm going to take him some flowers."

"I'll come with you," said Sven.

Clare and Sven went to the hospital, and found Trevor. He was lying in bed. He smiled when he saw them.

"Thank you for coming. I'm sorry to cause you trouble," he said.

"It's no trouble at all," said Clare. "Are you OK?"

"Oh yes, I'm fine. I want to go home. But the doctor won't let me. She wants to do some more tests."

"Can you walk?" asked Clare.

"Oh yes, I can walk very well, but the doctor won't believe me. I think she's a new doctor," said Trevor.

"You are going to miss your party," said Sven.

"I know. I told the doctor about the party. I asked her if I could leave the hospital, just for a few hours, but she said 'no'. I think she is too strict."

"Can't you just leave for a few hours, and then come back?" asked Sven.

Trevor shook his head. "The nurses will see me." Trevor looked around the room. "It is not a good start to my retirement, but at least I have my own room here, and my window opens onto the garden. It's nice and sunny too."

Clare and Sven looked out of the window. The room was on the ground floor, and it had a nice view of the garden and the roses.

"But the food is terrible. Really terrible. I was looking forward to the food at the Grand Hotel," said Trevor.

Clare looked at Trevor. He looked so sad. "We will visit you again soon Trevor," she said. "You just relax."

"OK, thanks for coming," said Trevor.

Clare and Sven went back to the office. They talked a lot that afternoon.

On Friday evening, Trevor had dinner and then switched on the TV. It was the worst meal he had had in hospital, and he didn't eat very much.

My party would have been today, he thought sadly. *Today would have been my last day of work if I hadn't had the accident. What a terrible start to my retirement!*

Then, someone knocked on the door.

"Come in!" he said.

Clare, Sven and another man he had never seen before walked into the room.

"Hello, this is a nice surprise," he said. "But who is this?"

"This is Charles, my grandfather. He looks like you. Don't you think?" said Clare.

Trevor looked at Charles. He was about the same age as Trevor, and he had short grey hair. He was wearing glasses.

"Well, I suppose he does a little, but…"

"Quick! Give Charles your pyjamas!" said Clare.

"Pardon?" said Trevor.

"Give Charles your clothes! He is going to stay in hospital tonight. And you are going to come to the party!"

"What? But…"

"There's no time to argue Trevor! Give Charles your pyjamas."

Sven took a suit out of a bag. "Your wife gave me your suit." He passed it to Trevor. "Quick! Get changed!"

Clare went out of the room. Trevor was very shocked, but he got undressed and gave his clothes to Charles. Charles got undressed, put the hospital clothes on, and got into bed.

Clare went back into the room.

"Thank you so much for doing this Charles," said Sven.

"Oh, it's no problem. I'm happy to have a night away from the wife! Peace and quiet at last!" He took a book out of his bag, and started to read.

A few minutes later, the nurse on the desk looked up and saw the three visitors come out of Trevor's room.

"How is he?" asked the nurse.

"Oh, he's fine. But he's very tired. He's gone to sleep," said Sven.

"OK, I won't disturb him tonight," said the nurse.

"Thanks, goodnight," said Clare.

They hurried out of the hospital and got into Clare's car.

"I can't believe I am doing this!" said Trevor.

Clare turned to him and smiled. "You didn't think you could miss your retirement party did you? Everyone is waiting at the Grand Hotel for you!"

"How will I get back to the hospital?" asked Trevor.

"We'll take you there tomorrow morning. Don't worry! Everything will be fine! Forget about it! You can worry about it tomorrow."

They arrived at the hotel. They walked into the party room. Everyone from the office was there. Trevor's wife and daughter were there too. Everyone started clapping and cheering. Trevor smiled. *I could come to my party after all. These people are great. I will miss them*, he thought. *Now, where is the food…*

6. A GREAT NIGHT OUT

"Good morning everyone," said Bevan Ashton.

The staff in the big insurance office stopped talking, and waited for Bevan to continue.

"I hope you all had a good weekend, but I hope you didn't party too much. We are very busy at the moment. I'd like to introduce our newest staff members. This is Adeena. Adeena Hussein. She will be working with you in customer services, Sandra."

Sandra nodded and said, "Hi, Adeena. Welcome."

"And this is Felix Ebo. Felix will join technical support, Fiona's group."

"Adeena and Felix are joining us because Noelle is transferring to our Leeds office, and Bernard is going back to Australia."

Bevan turned to speak to Adeena and Felix. "I'm sure you won't have any problems. Sandra and Fiona will show you what to do. But you can come and see me any time if you have any problems or questions."

"Thank you," said Felix.

"I'm sure everything will be OK," said Adeena.

"I'll leave you, then. Get back to work everyone!" said Bevan. He left the room.

Sandra got up from her desk and walked over to Adeena.

"Come and meet everyone. Noelle doesn't leave until Friday. She can explain her job to you," she said.

Fiona was sitting at the back of the big open plan office.

"Come down here, Felix! We're the computer experts! Bernard's

27

late for work as usual. But we can get you started on solving some problems anyway."

Felix smiled and walked towards the back of the office.

Adeena and Felix enjoyed their first week in their new jobs very much. The work was not difficult, and everyone was very friendly. Noelle helped Adeena learn how to talk to the customers on the telephone.

"I'm going to Leeds because my fiancé lives there," she told Adeena. "We're getting married next year. I'm going to miss Sandra, Beth and Tony a lot. You'll like working here. Everyone who works in customer services is nice."

Felix was working with Fiona, Ravi, Melanie and Bernard in technical support.

"We don't have any contact with customers," Fiona explained. "Our job is to keep the computer systems in this office running. We solve problems and sometimes we teach other staff members how to use new software."

Felix found technical support very interesting. The members of the team laughed and joked a lot. They also worked very hard when something went wrong. On Wednesday, there was a system failure and the technical support team worked until 2:00am on Thursday morning to fix it. At other times there was no work for them and they had some free time. Fiona did crosswords, Ravi played computer games, Bernard watched sport and Melanie wrote long emails to her boyfriend in France.

"You are good at your job," Fiona told Felix. "That's good. Bernard is a bit crazy and he's always late for work, but he is the best problem solver we have. I thought we would be in trouble when Bernard left, but I am sure you can do his job just as well."

On Thursday afternoon, everyone got an email from Sandra.

---Farewell party for Noelle and Bernard. Tomorrow after work. We'll meet in the pub across the road at 6pm. It will be a great night. See you there!---

Adeena was worried. She went to talk to Sandra.

"Sandra, about this party..."

"You will come, won't you?" said Sandra. "It's for Noelle and she wants you to be there. And we're joining up with technical support because Bernard is leaving too. They love to party! It will be a great night!"

"But, Sandra. I've never been to a pub. I don't drink alcohol. My culture…" Adeena was embarrassed.

"Adeena! You don't have to drink alcohol! Bevan doesn't drink, but he comes to the pub with us sometimes. Can you go to a place where other people are drinking alcohol?"

"Mmm. Yes. I think that would be OK."

"So come to the farewell party. You can drink fruit juice or soda. It's not a problem."

"Thank you," said Adeena. "I would like to come."

Adeena went back to her desk. Noelle was sitting next to Sandra. She had heard the conversation. Noelle and Sandra looked at each other. "Tony!" they both said at once.

"I'll talk to Tony," said Noelle. "You had better talk to Fiona. Those idiots in technical support have a strange sense of humour."

Noelle waited until Adeena went out to lunch, then she went to Tony's desk.

"Tony," she said. "Adeena is coming to my farewell party tomorrow night. She doesn't drink alcohol. So you must promise me that you won't play any silly tricks!"

"Like what?" asked Tony.

"Don't put alcohol in her fruit juice while she isn't looking! Don't buy her a vodka and orange juice and tell her it's just orange juice. It's not fair."

"I wouldn't do that," said Tony. "I like a joke, but not jokes like that."

"OK," said Noelle. "I'm sorry. I like Adeena. I don't think she has been to a party in a pub before. I want her to have a good time."

Sandra talked to Fiona. Fiona called her team together and said, "If any of you do anything silly, like putting alcohol in someone's drink when they are not looking, I will make sure that the next time we have a computer system problem on a weekend, the person who played the joke will be working Saturday and Sunday alone!"

"OK, OK, Fiona," said Ravi. "Felix and I will be good little boys!"

"Anyway," said Bernard. "Some people are allergic to alcohol. When I was at boarding school, someone put some Japanese sake in a boy's soda. He was very allergic to it and he almost died!"

On Friday at 5:30, the office was very noisy. Bernard was dancing around the office. He was singing, "We're gonna party, it's gonna be a party, hey, hey a party, who's gonna party…"

Tony joined in. "Who's gonna party, who's gonna party?"

"Quiet, you two!" shouted Fiona. "Wait until we get to the pub please! Some people have work to finish. No one can work with all that noise!"

Everyone left the office together at 6:00 and walked across the busy road to the pub. The bar was crowded but they found two tables in a corner and pushed them together.

"Good," said Sandra. "We've got ten chairs so that's perfect."

"I'll get everyone a drink," said Bernard. "What do you want to drink?"

Beer, beer, beer please," said Ravi, Felix and Tony.

"OK," said Bernard.

"Beer for me too, please," said Fiona.

"Melanie, Sandra, Noelle? What can I get for you?"

Melanie and Sandra wanted white wine and Noelle asked for a glass of cider.

"How about you, Beth and Adeena?" asked Bernard.

"Do they have cola?" asked Adeena.

"Of course they do."

"I'll have cola too," said Beth.

"OK that's five beers, two white wines, a glass of cider and two colas," said Bernard.

"Felix and I will come and help you carry them," said Ravi.

The three men pushed their way across the room to the bar. They soon returned with drinks for everyone.

Everyone talked and laughed. Fiona told funny stories about the problems the bosses had with the new computer software.

"My grandmother is better at using a computer than Bevan!" she laughed.

Tony and Ravi teased Noelle about her boyfriend in Leeds. Bernard tried to teach them some Australian expressions. "If you come to visit me in Sydney, you'll be stonkered if you don't know how to speak Strine."

"Sorry," said Felix. "I don't understand!"

"I'll translate for you, Felix," said Fiona. "Bernard said that you would be puzzled. You will not understand if you don't learn how to speak the Australian dialect. It's not true you know. Bernard is teasing you. Most Australians speak very good English!"

Bernard picked up his glass. "It's empty," he said. He seemed surprised.

"My turn," said Fiona. "Same again, everyone?"

Fiona came back with a tray of drinks. Then later, Tony bought some more. Adeena was surprised that Beth wasn't saying very much. She seemed very happy, but she wasn't talking. Sandra noticed it too.

"Are you OK, Beth?" she asked.

"Yes, I'm fine."

"But you're not drinking alcohol. Do you feel sick?" Sandra asked.

"Shh. No. I'm fine. But my husband and I are trying for a baby. We have been trying for a long time. And I think I might be pregnant!"

"Congratulations!" shouted Sandra.

"Shh," said Beth again. "I'm not sure yet. So I don't want to talk about it."

"OK, sorry," said Sandra. "But I'm very happy for you if you are pregnant."

"I'm hungry," said Ravi.

"You're always hungry," said Melanie. "But it's seven thirty. We should eat something before you all get drunk. Where shall we go to eat?"

They went to the Indian restaurant down the road from the pub. When they finished eating, Bernard said, "Where are we going next?"

Adeena was surprised. "Hasn't the party finished now?"

"No, no!" said Tony. "It's only nine o' clock. We can't go home yet."

"Sandra and I have a plan," said Fiona. "The Three Glasses pub on Marshbank Street is having a karaoke night. We're going there."

"Karaoke!" Felix was worried. "We have to sing! I can't sing!"

"Of course you can," said Melanie. "All of us are terrible singers but we sing anyway. It's fun."

So they went to The Three Glasses. The karaoke equipment was set up in a corner of the bar. There was a small stage, a microphone and a screen where the lyrics for the songs were displayed.

"We're all going to sing," said Sandra. "Now write your names down."

"Oh, no!" laughed Fiona. "You are not going to let Ravi sing are you?"

"Of course he can sing!" said Sandra. "Beth and I will sing together. Adeena you'll sing, won't you?"

"Yes. I will sing something." Adeena was happy. Usually she was shy, but she loved to sing. She sang at family weddings and birthdays. Her family thought she sang well. This would be her first chance to sing in public.

There were other groups of people in the bar as well. When they found some seats and sat down, three young women were standing around the microphone singing *Don't cry for me Argentina.*

Oh, thought Adeena. *They're very good. Maybe I shouldn't try to sing here.*

Other people got up and sang. Some were good, some were average and some were very bad, but no one cared.

Adeena noticed that when someone got up to sing, the people in their group watched and listened, but mostly, the other groups in the bar talked to each other and didn't take much notice. *It will be OK,* thought Adeena. *I like these people from my office. They're nice. I can sing for them.*

Finally, it was the turn of their group. Tony and Bernard got up and sang a Black Eyed Peas song. They sang very loudly and some other people in the bar joined in and sang with them.

Ravi sang *I did it my way.* He was a terrible singer and some people even booed. Ravi didn't mind. He smiled and bowed and said, "I will now sing another song…"

"No! No!" shouted Tony and Bernard. They went up to the stage and carried Ravi away. Everyone was laughing.

Noelle got up to sing. She didn't have a very good voice but she was a great dancer.

"This is fun, isn't it?" Felix said to Adeena. "I'm enjoying myself."

"Are you going to sing?" asked Adeena.

"Yes. I guess, I must sing something. Sandra said we all have to sing."

Beth and Sandra sang together, and then Fiona sang. Suddenly it was Adeena's turn.

"Oh no. I can't do this! I thought I could but I can't!" she said.

Tony pulled Adeena up out of her chair. "Yes you can! Look. Everyone's talking. The other people in the bar won't listen. Just us. You can do it."

Adeena walked up to the stage and took the microphone. Tony was right. At the other tables people were drinking and talking. A group at the back of the bar was singing football songs. No one was looking at her. She took a deep breath and started to sing. She sang *Tonight* from *West Side Story.*

Suddenly there was silence. Everyone in the room stopped talking and laughing and singing. Adeena had a beautiful voice. When she finished, everyone in the bar clapped. "More! More!" they shouted.

Adeena shook her head and dropped the microphone. She ran back to their table.

"Wow!" said Fiona. "You are amazing! Sing another one!"

"No! No!" Adeena was embarrassed.

Tony rescued her. "It's Felix's turn. Go on Felix!"

Felix sang an Elvis Presley song. He was very good. He imitated Elvis Presley very well.

Finally it was almost midnight. "I put my name down twice," said Bernard. "Come on everyone. We're all going to sing."

Bernard went to the microphone. He told everyone in the bar to be quiet. "We are all going to sing the last song! And it will be....*We are the champions!*"

The staff in the bar turned the music volume up very loud. Everyone got up and danced and sang together.

Then it was time to go.

As they were walking out the door, a man approached Adeena. "My name is Seth Walshingham. I own this pub. I also have a nightclub. You have a great voice. I'd like you come and sing there."

"No, no," said Adeena. "My family would never agree."

"Well think about it. I think you have a great talent. Here's my card. Think about it and call me!"

He gave Adeena his business card.

Out on the street Sandra asked Adeena. "Will you call him? I think you should."

"No. My family would be so angry. I like to sing for fun, not for money."

Adeena put the card in her wallet.

I'll keep the card as a memory, she thought. *Because it has been a great night out. A wonderful, exciting party night.*

THANK YOU

Thank you for reading Party Time! (Word count: 11,004) We hope you enjoyed the stories.

If you would like to read more graded readers, please visit our website http://www.italkyoutalk.com

Other Level 3 graded readers include
A Dangerous Weekend
A Holiday to Remember
Akiko and Amy Part 1
Akiko and Amy Part 2
Akiko and Amy Part 3
Be My Valentine
Different Seas
Enjoy Your Business Trip
Enjoy Your Homestay
I Need a Friend
Old Jack's Ghost Stories from England (1)
Old Jack's Ghost Stories from England (2)
Old Jack's Ghost Stories from Ireland
Old Jack's Ghost Stories from Japan
Old Jack's Ghost Stories from Scotland
Old Jack's Ghost Stories from Wales
Stories for Christmas
The Curse

Together Again
Who is Holly?

ABOUT THE AUTHOR

I Talk You Talk Press is a Japan-based publisher of language textbooks, graded readers and language learning/teaching resources.

Our team is made up of highly experienced language teachers and translators, who have all studied at least one additional language to an advanced level.

This experience enables us to design our materials from the perspective of both the teacher and the learner. We consult with both teachers and language learners when designing our textbooks and graded readers, and test our materials extensively in the classroom before publication.

We are a fast-growing press, and currently publish graded readers for learners of English. We publish new graded readers monthly.

www.ingramcontent.com/pod-product-compliance
Lightning Source LLC
Chambersburg PA
CBHW022348040426
42449CB00006B/781